THE LITTLE BOOK OF OLD WIVES' TALES

SARAH KLAIN

The Little Book of Old Wives' Tales by Sarah Klain
The Little Book of series vol. 1

Copyright © 2021 Sarah Klain

First printing edition 2021

All rights reserved. No part of this book may be reproduced, distributed, or transmitted in any form or by any means, including photocopying, recording, or other electronic or mechanical methods, without the prior written permission of the copyright owner, except in the case of brief quotations embodied in book reviews and certain other non-commercial uses permitted by copyright law.

This is a work of fiction. Places, events, and incidents are either the products of the author's imagination or used in a fictitious manner.

Library of Congress Control Number: 2021912368

Cover by Maxi Vittor.

Illustrations by M. Shohug.

Page design by Bryony van der Merwe.

ISBN 978-0-6452009-0-4 (hardcover)
ISBN 978-0-6452009-1-1 (paperback)
ISBN 979-8-2013-9627-5 (eBook)

Digital Marketing
Benjamin Payne at Fun Serious Creative Agency.

To all the fierce, strong women in my family. In particular, my mother and grandmother. Whom without these tales I would have no story. Thank you for your constant leadership, guidance, and encouragement in all that I do. And, to my dear father, for always supporting your girls.

Contents

Introduction 2

Premonitions 3

Relationships 17

Pregnancy 25

Death 31

Health 37

Misfortune 43

Fortune 59

Introduction

An old wives' tale is a traditional belief, story or idea said to hold truth and is superstitious in nature. They are considered wildly exaggerated and unverified urban legend or folklore, passed down through ancestry.

All tales documented in this book have been passed down through my Eastern European lineage from woman to woman, and generation to generation.

And so, the tales begin, *'It is said...'*

PREMONITIONS

If someone sneezes after or during a conversation, it is an affirmation of the truth.

Do not stare at a child too much or you will bring upon the evil eye to the child.

PREMONITIONS

Always wear a piece of red string on the left wrist. It will protect you against the evil eye.

If you wear your clothes inside out, you are going to be beaten.

PREMONITIONS

Never walk on or step over someone if they are sitting on the floor or they will not grow.

If you get a floppy handshake from someone and they avoid eye contact, they are deceitful.

PREMONITIONS

Should you remove any rings from your fingers, do not hand them directly to someone or you will both soon argue. Instead, place the rings on a flat surface for the other person to pick up. Return the rings in the same way.

If you hiccup, someone is talking about you.

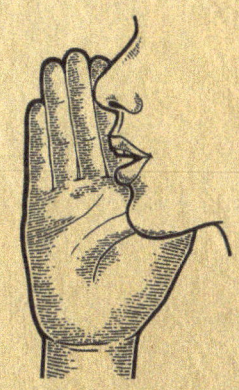

PREMONITIONS

If your left ear is ringing, someone is going to get in touch with you.

When leaving a friend's home, never open the door for yourself or you will not return to their house.

PREMONITIONS

Never break holding hands with someone over an object or it will cause a division between the two of you.

If you lend money to a friend, do not expect it back. You lent it; you did not give it.

RELATIONSHIPS

RELATIONSHIPS

If someone says, 'I love you' repeatedly, it is not true.

If the little and big hands meet on a clock dial by overlapping and falling onto one another, someone is thinking of you romantically.

RELATIONSHIPS

If a ladybeetle lands on your hand, and if you are single, ask, 'Where will I get married?' The direction it flies off in is the direction of your future groom.

If a groom does not drink alcohol, womanise, or gamble, it means he has some other hidden vices.

RELATIONSHIPS

When it rains on the day of a wedding, the bride will be unfaithful.

22

When you see a bride, touch your belly button for good luck.

PREGNANCY

If your stomach is higher during pregnancy, it will be a girl. If it is low, it will be a boy.

If your partner gains weight during pregnancy, he is having a sympathy pregnancy.

PREGNANCY

If you get spots or pigmentation

on your face during pregnancy,

it will be a boy.

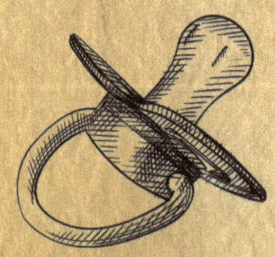

When a woman goes to the hospital to give birth, someone in the house must splash water behind the woman's departure to bring her good luck.

PREGNANCY

When rain is followed by sunshine, a witch just gave birth.

30

DEATH

𝒟o not walk around in socks. It may bring death upon your family, especially if your parents are still alive.

If you see a rainbow, it means

someone you know will pass

away soon.

DEATH

When it rains at a funeral, it allows the deceased to rest in peace.

One must never cry too much after the death of a person, or you do not let their soul rest.

HEALTH

To prevent or aid in the healing of mastitis, place cabbage leaves on the affected nipples.

If you get a stye, it is because you were looking where you should not have.

HEALTH

If you get a stye, gently rub a wedding band over it. It will heal fast.

40

If you get the hiccups, drink a glass of water upside down and your hiccups will stop.

MISFORTUNE

Walking under a ladder will bring bad luck.

Placing your hat on a table

will bring bad luck.

MISFORTUNE

Opening an umbrella indoors will bring bad luck.

Cheering with glasses of water

will bring bad luck.

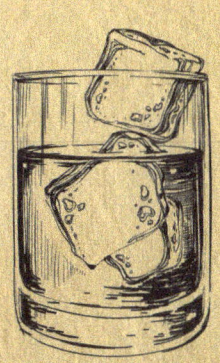

MISFORTUNE

If you spill salt, it will bring bad luck. Throw additional salt over your left shoulder to reverse it.

Do not cross the road when you see a black cat. It will bring bad luck.

MISFORTUNE

If you break a mirror, you bring seven years bad luck.

Do not whistle in the house or you will never have any money.

MISFORTUNE

If you buy medicine for a sick person, never take money in return or you will get bad luck and/or sick.

When someone is pouring you a drink, always make sure the glass is flat on a surface. If the glass is raised, you will be the very drunk one.

MISFORTUNE

If you leave the house and have forgotten something, never return to the house to get it or you will bring bad luck.

Never leave your purse, bag, or wallet on the floor or you will never have any money.

MISFORTUNE

An itchy right eye means you will cry or be upset.

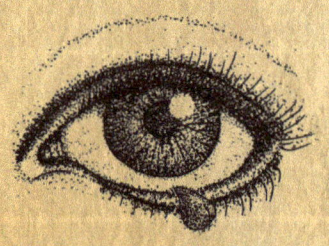

56

An itchy right palm means money will be leaving you.

MISFORTUNE

An itchy nose means you are going to be terribly angry.

FORTUNE

An itchy left eye means surprise and happiness will be upon you.

An itchy left palm means money is coming your way.

FORTUNE

An itchy left ball of the foot means you are going to travel or be up for a trip or adventure.

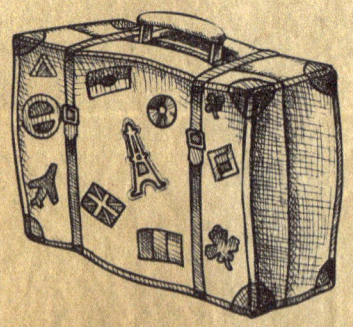

During a dry spell, beat some drums, walk barefoot, and wear a flower halo to bring in the rain.

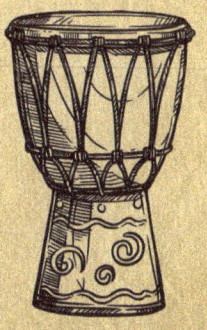

FORTUNE

If you have a fallen eyelash, put it inside your top and it will bring good luck.

64

If you eat garlic, you do not have to worry about bad witches.

FORTUNE

A four-leaf clover brings

good luck.

If you get pooped on by a bird,

it will bring money your way.

FORTUNE

If you step in dog poo, it will bring good luck and money.

68

If you see a tiny moon crescent in the sky, rub your head vigorously with a cash note whilst staring at the 'money moon'. It will bring you good fortune.

FORTUNE

If you gift someone a purse or wallet, ensure that there is already a coin inside. This will start them off with good fortune so that they can financially prosper.

About the Author

Sarah Klain is a Sydneysider and grew up by the water in Bondi Beach. After three decades of being raised with superstitions and old wives' tales, she finally decided to share her strange customs with the world.

When Sarah is not busy hopping over pavement cracks or ensuring she does not spill any salt, she works in the ethical artificial intelligence advisory field.

To find out more about Sarah, head to sarahklain.com, and @sarah_klain_writer on Instagram.

www.ingramcontent.com/pod-product-compliance
Lightning Source LLC
Chambersburg PA
CBHW061759290426
44109CB00030B/2891